Heterophobia

Poems by Ragan Fox

Faggot: For Gay Boys who Have Considered Rainbows when Suicide wasn't Enough originally appeared in <u>Freedom To Speak</u>, edited by Scott Woods, Debora Marsh, and Patricia Smith, © 2003.

If I Were A Woman originally appeared in <u>In Our Own Words Vol. 3</u>, edited by Marlow Peerse Weaver, © 2001.

ISBN 1-59021-019-0

Lethe Press
102 Heritage Ave
Maple Shade, NJ 08052
www.lethepress.com

Interior design by Sou MacMillan.
Cover photographs by Sara McKinnon.
Cover design by Sou MacMillan.

Manufactured in the United States of America.

For Daddy. I miss your pickle nose and beautiful blue eyes.
How about one more dance?

The author wishes to thank Steve Berman, Sou MacMillan, Sara McKinnon, and Lethe Press; Karma Chavez, Linda Park-Fuller, Belle Edson, Jennifer Linde, and Marty Yudizky; the slam poetry community, most notably Mike Henry, Regie Cabico, Phil West, Genevieve Van Cleve, Wammo, Patricia Smith, Buddy Wakefield, and Rachel Kann; Mom, Dwayne, Joyce, and Tina, for investing in my spirit and embracing my future instead of my past; and, of course, Daddy, your lap will forever be my proudest soapbox.

How to Break a Boy with Kisses

Accidental Marxist

No Head is Worth its Weight in Stone

Past Tense

I lust for straight men because heterosexuality is a fiction, and I live in fiction, the fictive discourses of my own life, past, present, future. To swing into the fulcrum is to challenge the fact/fiction binary, to discover the truth of fiction, to factualize the plot of my imagination.

—Fred Corey and Thomas Nakayama
Sextext

How to Break a Boy
With Kisses

Modern Plagues and Other Myths Regarding Natural Selection

Busy little bee,
before you fly,

be forewarned
that some winged-bugs pass

when their stingers
get stuck in the hides they stick,

and those followers of flowers
and princes of pollen

will never live to
stab another.

The pull of honey—
sweet and thick enough

for little buzzers
to battle bears,

but bee-ware where you stick
your stinger,

little bee,
bee-cause there are plagues
more dangerous than disease,

like love.

Shake the Baby

His fear of commitment is said to have first
wo-MAN-*infested*
from his breast pump
mom-a-lom-a-ding-dong and
then his wop-bop-a-doo-bop pop.

> *Baby has been shaken*
> *by modern plagues and other myths;*
> *didn't his lovers know better than to shake the baby?*
> *Baby is best served stirred,*
> *but never shaken.*
> *Never shake the baby.*

Despite past woes he knows that
if he wants to get a prime cut
he has to blow the butcher
of two men who will train him
to beg, roll over, and play dead,
the same way he taught me.

> *The baby who screams the least*
> *will get loved the most.*
> *Babies don't come with manuals.*

He wrote the book on me, though—
well, he cashed the advance
and scribbled a few notes on Post-its
left stuck to my bathroom linoleum.
Am I this transparent?:

I.
Know many useless facts:
The best way to get the honey bee into bed
is to speak to it on its level—
so, watch one football game a week,
one hour of CNN,
surf the web for 30 minutes,
go to an AA meeting once a month,
learn how to make really good salsa,
tell that bee,

"I don't watch TV"
and then make a face;
go to a few drag shows,
taste a few wines,
kiss a few asses,
and brush your teeth.

II.
Watch old Russ Meyer flicks;
plug in
Faster Pussycat, Kill! Kill!
Memorize choice lines,
insert in appropriate places
i.e., you go home with a bee
       that you met in a bar
              upon entering his honeycomb
say, "This is quite a play pen you got here, Buster!
       What you need now is a playmate!"
If he doesn't prick you with his sticker immediately,
swat him.

III.
After dating for a month
if he buzzes, "I love you"
he's probably infected with West Nile.
Once you've kicked him to another tree,
sit at home
listen to sad, sucky, sappy music,
go out to the bar,
meet another bee—
repeat as needed.

Did the baby love me
or was he silent because he was afraid
I would shake him?

Gay Bar Group: A Typology

Party fag is over-the-top. Her dog's name is "Scotch" and her cat's name is "Brandy." She, and by "she" I mean "he," slurs words and salivates down her own chin:
>I'm slo flucked up!

She'll share the most inane observations with you, like:
>My hands...smell like...a calculator (drunk laugh).

She spills more Cosmopolitan than she drinks. By the end of the evening, she *will* lose her blouse and by "blouse" I *do* mean "blouse."

The anti-thesis of party fag is designated driver guy. Designated driver does not want to be at the bar and he's not afraid to articulate his tap water-drinking wrath. His comments are peppered with yawns and attitude:
>(Yawn) I'm bored!

The minute you find a hot guy to talk to, designated driver will be up your ass. He's always got weird rules when it comes to men:
>We used to computer date, so you can't talk to him.
>Can we go?

Oh, you *will* put up with his shit, because he *drives*.

Straight male friend is like botched communication theory. He's a poststructuralist! He'll defend the *idea* of his heterosexuality until he's blue in the face, but it doesn't translate into the "real" world. "Straight" friend is the only guy in your "faggle" of men who will get any homosexual action that night. His amnesia the next morning is more nauseating than your hangover:
>Dude, what did I do last night? I don't remember anything. It hurts when I sit down though. Did I fall?

Although she's not a boy, fag hag, otherwise known as "fruit fly" or "fag nanny," is your Ellis Island to meeting new men. She's always dressed as if she's ready to enter a salsa bar or tango competition. She knows every man in the bar on a first name basis. Fag hag is the mayor of gay city. If she doesn't like you, she *will* have your ass arrested. She's fucking the cop at the door, the only legitimately straight man in the joint. She's *in love* with you but she doesn't *love* you.

Then, there's you and we all know how normal *you* are.

While the Boy Took a Bone

A Lust Story
A Tribute to GertrudeStein

While the boy took a bone. It only matters that the boy took a bone. As the boy took of a bone, the boy took a bone, a lust story.

While and during, and during or while, and during or, or while the boy took. While, but not before, and, or during or while the boy took the bone, and the boy took of the bone, a lust story.

In, not before, not before but in. In the moment before, before it was in. In in and around, but never before, but never before it was in.

Taking it in was the boy with his bone. The bone never took to taking it in. To take or to took or even to tooking, to take the took like never before taking the boy with his bone was taking it in.

It had to go. To go it had to, and before it went it had to go. And, and to go before, before it had to go, all the while knowing it was time to go, but to go while knowing, and knowing when to go, before knowing. To know to go without knowing.

Feeling it as have felt it or to feeling the feeling the feeling to feel, and feel or feel the feeling is what it is like to have felt it.

While the boy took the bone, having felt the feeling, while the boy took a bone, a lust story. A lust story, while the boy took a bone, a lust story.

Relax to relax, and to relax, relax or relax. To, and, to relax to relax while relaxing relax. After having relaxed, relax is to be relaxing.

And after, not before, and sometimes during while, but never before. Only during or after the boy took a bone. The boy took a bone, a lust story.

Fresh Meat

"Fresh meat,"
that's what he-man called me three times in a thirty-minute
   conversation
at the gay sports bar that had Michelle Kwan jumps looped via video on
   every large screen TV jacked into the juke joint between *Dynasty* re-
   runs.

"Fresh meat" is what I'll be known as for the next three months in
   Phoenix;
not to beat a dead filet,
but when I think of "fresh meat,"
I imagine game killed and skinned five minutes ago,
sweating blood and hung (like a horse) on a silver hook.

There's something strange about calling a potential suitor "fresh meat,"
especially when he already feels eaten inside out by maggots.
The queers have an affinity for meat.
We call our young, "chicken,"
and sharpen our incisors on our lovers' bones.

"Fresh meat," however, makes me think of a Jewish Deli doubling as a
   circumcision sweat shop— stay away from the pork!
It conjures up images of Jeffrey Dahmer taking pictures of a blind
   date, one foot popping out of a wood chipper
and a filet of pelvis collecting frostbite in the freezer.

Queer men, in all their rants and raves about oppression and
   objectification
should know better than to refer to a man like me as "fresh meat."
Gay men, in all their talk of political correctness,
should recant any claims that conflates a female with a fish.

These are the thoughts racing through my mind as I sit open legged in a
   gay sports bar with posters of a breastless Mary Lou Retton over its
   pink clothed pool table with a sign that reads "Be careful with our
   balls boys!" by the place you drop your change.

I've got something to say to all the carnivorous queer men with their
   hoofs pressed firmly against the decaying backs of their freshly killed
   prey hoping for a one-night romp with the skinny new boy from Texas
   who looks like he's just dying for a cum mustache!

I am not your meat!
I am not a ten-inch slab of salami waiting to slide into the home base
of your butter rolls!
I am not your fresh meat!
I'm sure that was a great pick up line in the institution,
and worked wonders on your last boyfriend who lived in a halfway
house, ate makeup, and owned a morbidly large collection of dolls
purchased from the Home Shopping Network,
but I'm not that kinda' gal.

Sitting in this bar that smells of piss and Pantene hair products,
I feel the urge to grab one of the fluorescent pink, cock-shaped pool
sticks from the wall,
and shove it into the brown eye of this butcher in gay men's clothing.

I refuse to be objectified by a queer man wearing an 808 State T-shirt
[and] while I MAY BE a complete dynamo in the sack,
you aren't invited to the taste test, pal!

This fresh meat isn't for sale!
My self respect is not on the menu!

"Fresh meat?"
Here's a forked tongue...
stick it in me, big daddy,
because I'm done!

121

If you were wondering how many lickety-split-licks it takes
to get to the gooey-fruity center of my soul
the answer is one-
-night stand #121 is a closet creature;
he's an ex-football player,
ex-army/fraternity dude,
and ex-hetero looking for some ex-citing action.

Approaching me at the bar,
contestant number one wants to buy me a Rolling Rock;
he's trying to lick-er me up and down.
He says his name is Jack—
off the subject, he claims he's an inTOElectual
who's inTOE making my TOEs curl.
I bat an *Aeon Flux* eyelash and say,
"Why don't you just cut to the Chevy Chase, flap jack?"
He says,
"Wanna' fuck?"
He's a romantic.

Back at my maxi-pad
he's looking at me
like I'm some young Johnathon Taylor Thomas porn kiddie fuck doll.
He tells me he wants to
cover my body in Yo-gay-plait yogurt and play "gay" with games like,
"Let's find the fruit."
One week ago,
having some man twice my age,
my age squared, square,
sitting in my apartment
saying these things
would have made me feel like Sharon Stone in *Basic Instinct*—
tonight it makes me feel like Sharon Stone in...*Sliver.*

Suddenly, I'm out of the mood
but in the next five minutes he comes up with about a hundred ways to
   lovingly refer to my butt hole:
He calls it my,
"Brown eye,
         my back door,
                  my circle-o-love,

>   my boygina,
>   my con-cave,
>   my Hershey highway,
>   my shit ditch,
>   my vessel waiting to be filled."

I tell him, "It's just my butt hole
take it for the night or leave it—
just don't rename it."
He says,
"Ew- ice ice baby;
you want some of this army/fraternity/football player cock?
Is that what you want?
You want to be my little sorority bitch, Roger?"
I say, "First of all,
my name is RAGAN
and secondly
I see thru you
you see/I see/you see
I see your game;
so Mary, Mary quite contrary,
slip out of your little lamb costume,
unzip your zippety zip zippers,
unpop your clippety cloppety clap clasps,
unhinge your grip on my bed posts
because you're not one night stand #1—
you're one night stand #121
and I'm going to write a poem about you
and if you're wondering why I have to slice and dice your pride
with my pippety poppety poe-
poe-po-E-TRY to understand
I only took you home
so I could write about you—
just like you only took me home for a piece."

What the Website Won't Tell You

Love!
You won't find it on gay.com—
that's for sure!

For the unaware,
gay.com is an online bath house,
where men with screen names rivaling "the_AssMaster"
battle for my electronic affections on Sunday nights,
sending me pictures of their poc-marked and pimply penises
in the hopes that we will make a love connection,
but you don't find love on gay.com—
just cock-hungry, middle-aged hucksters looking for nooners with boys
    young enough to be their sons.

They'll try woo their way into your heart with such searing pickup lines as
"My spunk would look great on your face!"
That's just GREAT!
Nothing says "I love you" like male ejaculate flying into your eye!
Love!
It's all fun and games until somebody glues your eye shut!
THAT is a Hallmark moment!

As I sit
bare-assed on a slip covered chair in my living room,
talking to a 45 year old visiting masculine wrestler into vanilla and kink
who repeatedly tells me he's getting "all 'elmery' down there,"
I am reminded of Cinderella singing,
"Some day my prince will come!"
but I'm not Cinderella.
In fact, lately I've been getting less action than a condom machine in a
    convent.

Now, I've never met an actual gay.commer in the flesh,
and if I did,
I certainly hope he wouldn't open up a conversation with leading
questions like
"Can I pee on you?"
No, thank you.
Rain check?

This is the reality of gay online dating!

I may have crapped out in this sordid little game of love,
but I will never be so desperate that I compromise good sense for a roll
   in the hay with a visiting, balding, self-proclaimed "chicken hawk"
   from Toronto—
even with his pending offer to poop on my chest.

In my book,
"love" is not a word you write with yellow letters in the snow.
Where I'm from,
consummating a relationship does not involve leather, poppers, and a
   sling.
Call me old fashioned!

So, yes, some day your prince may come,
but if you met him on gay.com,
let's hope it's not in your eye.

Urban Legend

I've tried to sleep my way back into your bed.
Each trick I have up my sleeve is a piece of you stuck with spit on
  another man's skin.
Last night's lover had your eyes,
the night's before stole your thighs,
I've licked your forearm on a foreman,
and caressed your sun-kissed shoulders hijacked by a killjoy cop in a
  California crack house.

The puzzle is in putting you back together again.
All the pieces I've pulled don't seem to stick.
I've got two of your right middle fingers,
but the left is left out of reach.
I nearly let a man gut me like a fish for a freckle,
but the bruises left in his wake make it hard for me to...

You were the first to tell me the urban tale of men waking up in ice
  with missing organs,
and I'm starting to see sense in the story.
I turn men cold with a kiss and steal what I can,
because each cut I make into a stranger's skin brings me a hair, nail,
  and artery closer to being with you again.

I will fuck my way into oblivion,
stealing more than kisses on my way,
madly sewing spleen and sockets,
thinking no monster was ever more beautiful than Frankenstein,
and no fool more lonely than the one who created him.

David Cart-wrong

You have the
Smallest Penis
I have ever seen or
Smelt or felt and the
Ugly kind of small too
Kind of like Yoda
But without that wisdom
At the piercing
Parlor when they
Popped   your
Persistence   by
Persuading   you
Your prick was too
Pretty to pierce that
It was exquisite they
Meant it was exquisitely
Small   and   a   Prince
Albert prodded thru your
Petite prick would have
Proven petty to say the
Least and when we're
Speaking of your penis
I do mean the very least
You   see   Y o u r
Pride   your   Prick   and
Your piercings   Bug me   and
Not in a Jennifer Love Hewitt I Still
Know What You Did Last Summer sorta'
Way but in a Pam   Anderson Lee crab
Infested panty-   Hose get out of
My trailer   park and
Off of   my

Tommy Lee
before I flame out on your ass dimension
and honey
what's going on with the scary, hairy, milky mole pimple thing going on
at the end?
Is that supposed to be an eye-
-love making fun of your small penis;

your small penis is the stuff poems are made of—
at least this one-
-of my favorite things about your penis
is its high hanging balls-
-to the wall every time somebody mentions "family jewels"
because your penis is more like a family *rhinestone*, cowboy.

When they speak of innies and outties
I think they're referring to your belly button and not your penis
but I do have to admit
there is a particular poetic irony
that lies and flies between your milky thighs,
the fact that your body projects an outtie belly button
but an innie penis.
My question to you:
When your piece ceases to remain an outtie,
can you still
in good faith
call it a prick?
Surely, our modern vernacular
Is *more than meets the eye;*
surely, the *deceptacon* of your penis would *transform* into a more fitting term;
one comes to mind,
perhaps instead of a pe-nu*ss*,
we could call it a pea-nuT.

You see,
when you saw me recite my
poe-
poe-
po-E-tree
and pleaded with me:
If I ever got mad at you
not to portray you in some type of craptacular manner in my future poems;
you may as well have handed me a sword
and given me first class directions to your heart
FUCKER!
Think twice before you screw over a man
who uses a pen as his defense
and a voice as your vice,
because my pen
and my voice
only serve as a magnifying glass

which exemplifies how small your penis is.

And one last thing,
your ass is hairy too
but I'll get to that in David Cartwrong Poem #2.

Fifty-two Pieces

This poem was almost never written

because it was already written in your star-fucked eyes
because from the first time we met...
because...
because...
because...
because there are 52 pieces of me
                    you have never seen
                              fractured & shattered & crashed
                         crumpled up pieces of a fortune cookie fortune
              too difficult to read

                         but please try

because your mouth is a metaphor
              your eyes, science fiction
                    your penis, the cutest little haiku any mouth wrapped its
                    way around;

because I never got to tell you any of this
because I was so afraid of so many things
              falling in love
                    falling out
                         having the power
                                        sharing a bed
                                   my aching head
                    my aching head
         my aching head;

because blow-jobs
because job loss
because train track marks billowing up and down my bony arm
because his manhood billowed inside me
because ? begets ? begets ?
because you said you loved me
because I believed in that
because you lied
because → because → because
because my brother used to fondle me

because I fondled the bartender
because you still had one foot in the closet door
because I am damaged goods
because you won't return my phone calls
because when opportunity knocked I didn't answer the door
because we never fucked
because your kiss was more precious to me than...
because I want you back more than I want anything in the world
because not a day goes by that I don't think of you

>   my body
>   my soul
>   my aching head.

> Sweep me up,
> cut your fingers on the sharp and jagged pieces,
> dispose of me
> and the 52 pieces
> you
> will never see.

What Helen Must Have Thought

You said I needed to change,
so I moved to the upper East side,
like a killer WASP
with cornflake wings made of old Bud Light labels
stuck onto my back with
the same guts, glue, and determination they use to stick heels back
  onto a defunct pair of Jimmy Choo's.

When I lived on your palm,
right by a forked and crooked life line,
I was certain I could tell the future,
but there are things I was never able to read,
like your eyes
when they clouded over with the premonition of another man.

I'm sorry I can't read cards like you decipher the Egyptian route that
  leads to the end of us.

I'm spun too tight in paper cloths,
conserving the skin of what once was
in a room
in a pyramid
that oracles, yet to be born,
will swear to be cursed.

Some myths deserve to break through baby boys with bound feet,
  ambitious young men with feather wings held together with hair
  wax, and monsters in a maze you've created.

I am the opposite of the woman with snake hair—
stone turned to flesh,
and I will not go back.

I love you more than blind men making prophecies on a March day that
  will last longer than our first kiss,
but I won't go back.
I won't go.

Fortune Cookie Say

Gay sex isn't all about slings and fisting
poppers and unzipping zippers to unleash a one-eyed beast.
It ain't always about steamy scenes of cock-sucking
nipple-twist, ooh-la-la, mangled butt fuck, crabby crawlers sifting
    through a tropical pubie box.
Don't let the ass-slaying scenes of tumescent Roma tomato cock heads
    dupe you into thinking gay sex is a tic-tac-toe of crotch-bobbin',
    slurpy staffs of sexuality pounding in and pulling out
pump
pump
prostate bursting in a proverbial sea of ecstasy.
It's not all *Queer as Folk*, bathroom sex with straight boys, and sucking
    face with guys in high glossy Abercrombie ads.
Sometimes, gay sex ain't nothin' more than a half-hearted hand job
    from your older, creepy second cousin.

The seductive television shows that pull you in with the promise of
    hot, straight actors playing mixed up gay ghetto-homo aspiring
    heterosexuals be/lie the ties that I have to gay culture.
Gay sex isn't always kink, leather mask-wearin' men, whips, studded
    collars and beefcakes.
Sometimes it's waiting weeks for HIV results,
counting clocks that are ticking backward in time,
looking at a silent floor for answers,
praying to un-suck half the lousy cocks you've taken down;
looking at the floor,
making wishes;
peering at the ground
to find brightness
but you can't look down at the stars, Galileo Galilei.

After an all-night tear-fest at a tragic Chinese BBQ pit-o-despair,
I cracked open a fortune cookie with a hard head.
It read:
People die
Big Quilt
Angels in America isn't just a play;
it's a friend.
Gay man's heart broken open
like egg
or fortune cookie.

There are some fortune cookie fortunes not worth reading,
test results that can literally drain the life right out of you,
some slippery noodles are not worth the fight of chopsticks.

Gay sex isn't all about lube, dudes, beach parties on Fire Island,
    Provincetown, and pruning your man-bush;
It's not all about biting down on ears, whispering lies that sound like "I
    love you!"
bathroom stalls that double as brothels, and using beach towels as
    clean-up rags.

Gay sex isn't always sexy;
sometimes it's decay, waste, pain, and deadpan expressions—
bedpans and laughing past tragedy.
Sometimes it hits so close to home that you think you're wearing ruby
    slippers, Dorothy,
but no matter how many times you click your heels
you can't save him
and despite your own squeaky clean and sterile negative status,
you can't save yourself,
because, sometimes, gay sex isn't nearly as sexy as it sounds.

My Secret Skill

I know things the contestants on *Jeopardy* don't,
like how to break a boy with a kiss
then brush the hair away from his eyes
then build him back up from clay
      then kiln
          then fire
              then paint.

I know things they won't teach you in History books,
like how to break a boy with kisses,
then heat
      then smolder and smoke
          then grenade
              then pin
                  then aim
                    then heart
                      then explosion.

I know jokes comedians don't dare tell,
like how to break a straight boy's resistance in seven shakes of a lambs
   tail
with a single kiss
then meat
      then hook
          then sell
              then cook
                  then digest
                    then heart attack.

I see the truth in the weather report;
I can predict sunny days or make hurricanes blow in
with a pucker of my swollen lips,
I can turn the Grand Canyon into a Great Lake
then bathe
      then unplug
          then drain
              then boy
                  then lips
                    then kiss
                      then broken.

I break boys with my kisses,

and the sign in the store claims
I have to buy what I break,
but I'm broke myself;
to own these lips,
you'd have to be.

I cried when I had no shoes, until I met a man who had no feet; then I laughed...really hard.

—Jerri Blank
Strangers with Candy

Accidental Marxist

Kate, the Cursed

It's a shame, they said, *how the amber from her cigarette now burns brighter than the fire she carries within.* She was once Kate, they quipped, *Kate, the Wicked; Kate, the Cursed; Kate, the Shrew; now, she is just Kate. I fear, however, waves crash behind her eyes, and when she finds herself again, we all shall pay.*

*

And, so, Bianca took a shotgun to her sap-heart sister while she heated up a microwave dinner for the man who tamed her. And when the man who tamed her threw Kate's torn up body out to sea and found a new fire to fuck and put out, Bianca gathered her sister's scattered pieces on an ocean floor, and scotch taped her back together. All fragments of Kate were recovered with the exception of her four-part, faulty heart.

Perhaps, thought Bianca, *this is a blessing. It was her heart that led her astray to begin with.*

This is how Kate walked, for six days and seven nights. Once the formidable bride of Petruchio, she was now the postmodern bride of Frankenstein, stitched together with school supplies. Her life became a talk show. She lived in green rooms & smiled when she was told to smile & applauded when the signs telling her to do so lit up & charmed the press in the wake of wicked blowing in. Hurricanes blew in the fleshy hole that once held her beating, pulsing engine, a mixture of cold and warm fronts in a space now consumed only by air, where fronts are oft born.

*

Have you seen Petruchio's latest piece of ass? a man at a bar asked his comrade. *She was a stripper before he found her, a young black girl addicted to white clouds until the cold man gave her a warm place to stay. She is a fine piece of ass,* the man explained, *but she's no Kate.*

And she isn't
nor could she ever be:
Kate, the cursed
Kate, the shrew
Kate, the kissed

Kate, the wife
Kate, the suburban homemaker
Kate, the woman who takes it up the ass for her husband's boss
Kate, the GOD DAMN Stouffer's dinner is burnt again!
Kate, the coke addict
Kate, the girl who was blown into oblivion by her sister's shotgun,
and carefully pieced together again.

Kate is coming after you Petruchio
I see her now
walking down the icy street that leads to your house
adhesive freezing & falling off
limb by limb, she comes undone
an arm
a toe
an ear
a finger
she leaves a trail of carnage, her own
as you and your friend fuck your newer and younger girlfriend
I see her as her sister trails behind her
scotch tape firmly in hand
sticking what she can back together
so.that.justice.will.finally.be.done.

Suburbia

Let's move to the suburbs,
get micro-perms,
wear coulats with fish prints,
and shave our pubic hair until we have bald beavers.

Let's move to the suburbs,
become Republican,
and download pictures of George Bush on the Internet/nude/doing
    coke/with Laura holding a whip,
e/lec/tro/cu/ting peo/ple <zzzzzzzz!>

We can become washed-up soccer moms with dishpan hands,
and do carpools to our Tupperware parties;
we can join the PTA—
"It doesn't matter if we don't have kids";
we have psychological problems,
and husbands that are assistant managers at Baby Ga!P!
We'll down shots of Crown for breakfast;
it's fun to drink!
It's fun to drink in the suburbs!

I have an overactive thyroid!
The most exciting thing to happen to me last year was my best friend's
    yeast infection!

I hate the big city!
It's evil;
they have people
that walk
on the street.
It's so dangerous!

I feel so safe here—
almost like I'm in a tiny bamboo box with no breathing holes
    <gasp, gasp, ga...>
Why don't you come move next door to me?
We'll be a coked up and cock hungry version of Lucy and Ethel!
We can swap recipes,
plant gardens together,
and have a kinky lesbian relationship

while our husbands play golf and jerk each other off!

I think my dentist fondles me while I'm "under."

Do you mind if I ask you a personal question?
Do you enjoy baked goods?
Because that's what we're all about here in *the burbs*—
lots of barbecue and baked goods,
and pills,
lots of pills!
I love pills!
Do you have pills?
Gotta' have pills!
The pills. Make the time. Tick. Away.

My husband has a small penis with a uni-ball,   and sleeps with the baby sitter,
which is strange   because we don't have kids,   but we do have lots of little
singing birds here in the burbs!   Sometimes   the birds talk to me!
They tell me to do things   like,   "Chirp, chirp.   Kill him.
Chirp.   Kill your husband.   Chirp, chirp.   KILLLLL HIMMMM!"
I love that song!   It's a catchy tune!

        Have I told you how my dentist fondles me while I'm under?

It's a picture perfect life here;
we just adopted a 3-legged Labrador Retriever—
we call him Tripod;
he has bad breath and a nasty bite,

like my
          husband hits me across my
                         dentist fondles me while I'm
                                      fending off my husband's p
                 U   n
                               C
                               hes
                                      me in the stomach
                                      pains from all the abuse.
I love it here in h
                 E
                 L
                 L
                 p me out and move next door
                               frame bashing against my

The house next door is for sale!

Psyche at the Trigger

Psyche lived in silent times;
she had nothing to say,
and she was saying it,
sitting in her rocking chair,
bound and gagged,
big toe firmly placed against trigger;
"This is how he has me sit during the day,"
her eyes would say
as she silently sat and watched her stories.

Two months ago,
she had been the beautiful deaf girl in the kissing booth,
working for tips at Caesar's Palace when he first spotted her,
the way he spotted so many like her,
and that night,
as she walked to her Nissan under the sleek Nevada moon,
she thought in signed language,
"Tonight is not a night to worry,
tonight is not a mace-laden night"
and as she drank this moment in,
he came from behind her,
drug her by her golden locks to his van,
brought her back to the bad place and explained the gruesome
situation,
so fast
so fast
so fast her eyes
could barely
read
his lips.

* * *

Eros was the Norman Bates of Greek mythology.
Growing up, he would dress in his mother's spiked heels,
rub her red lipstick against the protruding pink flesh protecting his
   sharp teeth,
and conceal his cock between skinny legs.
Eros was never happier than in these moments
until mother would quietly creep into his room,
and find her son,

and beat her son,
and humiliate him,
the way so many of her male friends did,
but mother never ripped him open,
never took him from behind and ripped him head to toe—
never clipped his angelic wings—
mother was not as equipped as her brethren.

* * *

He beats her at night now,
in those tender moments
she can take her toe from trigger,
and pop the joints in her feet.

He climbs her spine,
bites down on her ear and whispers,
"Mother thinks I should get rid of you now.
What do you think of that, little girl?"

She has nothing to say,
she says it loud,
and he likes
what
he
does
not
hear.

* * *

That day,
She was sitting in her rocking chair,
bound and gagged,
big toe firmly placed against trigger.

That day,
when the police huffed and puffed and blew down the bad man's house,
she looked up at the men, confused,
"This is how he has me sit during the day,"
her eyes said,
and these men,
who have seen it all,

get paid to be strong,
knelt by the girl and cried,
and, three weeks later, it was the most difficult task these men have
   encountered to conjure the courage to tell her Eros had fled.

* * *

I have seen her,
wandering city streets,
searching for her captor.

She has nothing to say,
and she says it...
in her eyes, bruised thighs, and swollen feet.

When she finds him,
she will pick up the sawed off shotgun
once super glued to her big toe,
and sign "Psyche at the trigger"
in broken A.S.L.

She has nothing to say,
and she is saying it well
as she blows him into a billion pieces
the way he blew so many of his mother's forgotten male friends,
and it will rain arrows that day,
February 14th,
Ero's arrows,
piercing hearts,
and paying the price
of love's sick.

Unsent Letter to the CEO of Hooters

Oh, Mr. CE-O,
I found a thongy in my Chinese chicken salad,
and when I complained to the girly girl
wearing her fuck-me heels and Lee press-on personality,
she shimmy shaked her way away like I hadn't said a damn thing.

Oh, Mr. CE-O,
I just wanted Ginger to talk to me,
to open her legs right up and tell me what was on her mind.
I wanted to kiss her full on the lips.
I wanted the service you promise in posters,
but all I got was a thong in my crunchy wanton Chinese chicken salad.

Oh, Mr. CE-O,
Ginger says she's just flinging meat to work her way through college,
but I don't think that's so.
Why, Mr. CE-O, is it that Ginger isn't on the menu?

Please tell Ginger you'll fire her,
put her baby back (ribs) on a spice rack,
and 86 her jiggle giggle if she doesn't spread her legs and let me kiss
   her full on the lips.

I think your server has a real attitude problem.
I want you to know that I've been dining at your establishment,
feasting on wanton women strip steaks for years.

If you don't let me bend her over and shove her in the oven,
I will sue!

Oh, Mr. CE-O,
the customer and the price is right,
and I promise that if you don't cave, man,
I'll talk to someone higher up,
so that I can go down below.
Mr. CE-O,
please put the Ginger strip steak on the menu
before you make me go
to Denny's.

Ten Reasons Why I Hate the ~~Fat Bitch~~ Who Always Sits in My Section at Romano's Macaroni Grill

10) Because she always make me list the fifty-eight low-fat items on the menu and then orders something like "chicken parmigiana with extra cheese and extra sauce and instead of the vegetable medley can I get a baked pot-at-o with extra sour cream and butter? Oh, I love butter. Lots of butter!"

9) Because when she comes with her friends, there's nothing more daunting or cheap than waiting on a six top of hungry ~~fat bitches~~.

8) Because she never orders alcohol—just water and then mixes it with lemon wedges and Equal—something she claims is a family recipe—it's called lemonade, ~~rolly-polly,~~ and we serve it.

7) Because if you're not paying for bread, don't make me get you a new loaf every five seconds. Other people like to eat bread, too! Share! Let some other customers have a loaf! It's their turn!

6) Because when she comes with her parents, three people sharing one dinner salad just doesn't make sense. I realize you don't want to have to actually absorb anything healthy into your system, but I think the three extra sides of Ranch dressing I've gotten for you have pretty much turned that salad into a junk food item.

5) Because it's just t-t-tacky to drink water with a straw.

4) Because it can't possibly be your birthday every time you come into the restaurant! I realize a free dessert is pretty tempting but don't ya' think I catch on? And every time you ask me to do it, you wink, like it's our little game! But it's not! I don't like the game! You win!

3) Because you're really not supposed to stick your finger into the desserts on the dessert tray to figure out which one you want for your fifth birthday this week- other people look at that tray too and now I have to take five minutes out of my time to replace the presentation dessert you destroyed with you "taste test." Five minutes longer that it's going to take me to get your dessert. Five minutes that you are going to bitch to my manager because your dessert wasn't on the table fast enough and you were huuuuuuunnnnngry!

2) Because once I actually saw her steal food from a baby in my section and then brag about how easy it was.

1) Because I understand that the only man who would ever be nice to you would be gay, but I don't appreciate you telling me how much you love the "gays" in front of my other tables.
~~FAT BITCH~~!

The Back

-coauthored by Sara Sutterfield Winn

Both: Welcome to the mystical magical world of Retail!
Sara: Can I help you with that?
Ragan: Can I squeeze you into it?
Sara: Cinch it?
Ragan: Clinch it?
Sara: Help you pick it out,
Ragan: pick it up,
Sara: pick your nose,
Ragan: or maybe I'll just go look for it in...
Both: THE BACK.

Sara: Excuse me, miss, but do you have this in a size 4 in...
Both: THE BACK?
Ragan: I'm looking for the first edition of Shakespeare's *Hamlet*; do
         you think you'd have it in...
Both: THE BACK?
Sara: I'm on the search for mankind's place in the great scheme of
             things,
         the meaning of life,
         the source of the universe,
         world peace,
Ragan: my foreskin,
Sara: and my dark haired, dark eyed,
Ragan: hung like a grizzly bear
Both: soul mate,
Sara: and I'm pretty sure you have him in...
Both: THE BACK.

Ragan: The BACK is the place where the magic happens.
         The BACK is the warehouse of all that is missing in your life.
         The BACK is where you should be. Imagine:
Sara: Row after row of clothing in size 26,
         box after box of size 11 shoes,
         crate after crate of happiness, joy and comfort.
Ragan: Your mother's milk?
Sara: It's in the BACK.
         Your old Teddy Ruxpin?
Ragan: It's in the BACK.
         That old issue of *Tiger Beat* featuring Screech from *Saved by
            the Bell*, and highlighting the career of Joey Lawrence?

Sara: Whoa! You won't find it out there; that's for sure.

Both: See, we hide it.
Sara: Retail employees laugh over your old blankies, the perfect shoe, the Cliff Notes to the book you have a test on tomorrow, the dress that will make them love you...
Both: THEY'VE GOT THE LIFE YOU SHOULD HAVE HAD...
        IN THE BACK.

Ragan: Beware, the BACK is not for everyone.
Sara: Fundamentalist Right-wing Christians are not allowed in the BACK,
Ragan: Kathie Lee Gifford is not allowed in the BACK,
        both Latoya and Tito Jackson are not allowed in the BACK.
Sara: If you're homophobic, racist, a misogynist, or watch
Both: *Walker: Texas Ranger*
Sara: for kicks,
Ragan: take the blue pill—
Both: the BACK is not for you.

Ragan: In the BACK, when an employee cheerfully asks, "Can I help you find something?"
        she's not afraid you're going to steal;
        she really wants to help you.
Sara: Boys with mullets named Skipper, and girls sporting camel toes named "Cherysh with a 'Y'" are not allowed to work in the BACK.
Ragan: They're not even allowed to go toward the door that leads to the BACK of the store.
        That's why they're called "greeters."
        At a store, a greeter is only one step above broken mannequin; in the future, they'll be replaced with robots wearing wigs who don't mind saying, hand on hip,
Sara: "Hi, how are you?"
Both: over and over and over
Ragan: eight hours a day,
        seven days a week,
Both: for the rest of their mechanical lives.
Sara: They will die at the front of the store
        and we will throw a party
Both: but the party will be in the BACK.

Ragan: The back contains a cure for cancer, AIDS, and meningitis,
Sara: an unlimited supply of pot and clean fuel,

Ragan: the perfect poem that's always on the tip of your tongue.
Sara: Marilyn Monroe, James Dean, and Dick Cheney—
not dead;
Both: they're in the back and we cannot lie;
you other brothers might deny...

Ragan: Now, I've been to the back
and it's no Eden;
Sara: it's the apple—
the false promise:
Ragan: A better book,
Sara: a better nose,
Ragan: a better lover,
Both: a better life!
Sara: Grab all you can off the displays and shove it down your pants
if you have to
Ragan: because all the merchandise is up front
Sara: and with a little creativity
Ragan: and just the right belt,
Both: IT WOULD BE SO YOU!

The Accidental Marxist

Additional Reasons we Should Consider you for Employment:

I'm a card carrying member of a new minority group, the terminally unemployed. I'm an accidental Marxist, subversive by sucking ass at finding gainful employment.

FACT: EMPLOYERS CRAVE EXPERIENCE THE WAY CRACK ADDICTS CRAVE COCAINE.

They fidget around in their black patent pleather swivel chairs and ask, "Wh- wh- what kind of experience do you have, Ragan?"

"I don't know; exactly what type of experience would you be looking for/for flower salesman at nightclub? I've never actually sold roses or Tic Tacs at a bar before, but I'm sure, with just the right training, I could be your man!"

[and] I'm sorry, but I don't think it takes multiple degrees in engineering, and summer internships at NASA to fold second hand shit stained jeans and "free Winona" T-shirts at The Buffalo Exchange!

Why in the world am I always interviewed by Shalle Corley, the evil HR troll with the cross-eyed cats; Shalle cuts out Kathy cartoons, and sticks them on the fridge in the "give me a fucking break" room? Shalle tells me I look young for my age, and I want to ask her, "Am I being carded for cigarettes, or is this an actual JOB INTERVIEW?" but unless I want to end up on the side of the street, holding a squigee, spitting on people's windshields, clutching a sign that says, "Why lie? It's for beer." I have to woo Shalle Corley, laugh at all her cat jokes, when all I really want to do is stick the big black cock of death in her mouth and <gun shot>!

Maybe this is why I'm working at Romano's Macaroni Grill in Westlake Hills again. I'm the Barbara Streisand of the restaurant industry; each time I retire, they find a way to suck me back in, and that's just about the time my customers start complaining about my lackluster attitude and lack of flair— that's just about the time I.melt.down. I say to them, "Go ahead and complain to my manager. Bitch until you're blue in the face! Last night, I held her hair back as she puked up Red Bulls & Vodka in a gay bar bathroom so somehow I don't think your complaint is going to affect my working situation that much!"

See, I have other things to worry about, namely using my Masters degree as spare toilet paper, because wiping your ass with cushiony softness is at the bottom of the needs pyramid when you're making $2.13 an hour shoveling cheap Italian crap down Michael Dell's wife's throat!

I'm sorry if this doesn't fit into your squeaky clean "additional reasons we should consider you for employment" box, but I'm not sorry I won't sell my soul to the highest bidder. I'm not sorry I won't be your industry butt boy. I'm NOT SORRY I can't be the 401K fuck wad you want me to be! So, just suck on it!

I Beg to Differ

So, I lost my temper;
went wacko, freaked out, blood pumping to temples, eyes glazed,
   fingers turned to fists, nails digging into torso, tongue forked,
   FUCKING PISSED off and on (and not in the good way)—
I lost it—
ripped out chunks of punk-dyed hair, talked myself purple, pleaded
   with sense- and earless men, crossed my eyes, cried into pillows,
   cursed your names to uncaring gods, sharpened knives, cleaned guns,
   crawled into spider holes, coiffed, re-coiffed, caffeinated myself,
   cleansed my colon, and meditated on the Hebrew letters for this
   throbbing disdain to feign apathy...
...but it won't.

You simply bring out the worst in me!
That's...why...I...lost...my...temper!
That's why I went a little crazy-eyed when the straightest, whitest guy
   in TEMPE told me I don't know homophobia when I'm staring it in its
   sorry ass face.
If I had been more articulate at the time,
I would have told him how making statements like the barnyard-ass
   bullshit he fed me reveals that he is aesthetically broke, busted,
   botched and bruised—
how DARE you assume I can't pin the tail on hate, Tempe CRACKER.

My temper, however, has simmered, sizzled down to a carcass in the
   months I've been away,
so now I can ar-tic-u-late my way through your hate.

Poetry isn't always a big fat fucking chuckle, bunch of brain dead
   beatniks tokin' ha-shish out of the happy bowl—
sometimes it's pain, love, loss, venting, anger, bewilderment,
   documenting the stories betwixt and between humanity.

Yes, sometimes, it is Matthew Shepard and gay bashing,
funerals that come too early, cracking knuckles, and commemoration.
Sometimes the point isn't found in a dime store punch line that you
   stole off a Bill Hicks album, CRACKER man.
Sometimes the point is bent out of shape, confusing, heart-wrenching,
   and stops you in your gaping track marks—just like life:

As I trek up three flights of steps to my apartment,

I hear a child scream "faggot" to the moon.
Just as I convince myself that his vitriol is spit elsewhere,
I am greeted by another young voice through a window screen singing,
"Hey, gay man."

I have taken more than my fair share of sucker punches for loving men—
the words "queer" and "faggot" have been branded on my body with
    uncaring tongues that double as whips—
snap
snap
Two guns have been pointed at my head by men targeting faggots to rob,
and while those thieves may have clawed my pockets dry,
I am rich in what I know.

I may not know how to keep cool under pressure;
in fact, I lose "it" more often than I should.
I don't know how to keep calm, breathe in, breathe out, bastion of
    light and serenity, count to ten backwards, wear a smiley face when
    it's being spit on, shake hands with the devil, make deals that drain
    me of integrity, read poetry when I'm not in the mood, and have my
    sincerity critiqued by men who write trite spite.

I don't know those things,
but, sucker cracker ass, I know homophobia
and while I clearly appreciate how your words have inspired me to
    meditate on just how naïve I may be when it comes to queers getting
    bashed with fists, guns, and words,
believe me, I know hate, cracker jack, and as fate would have it, I'm
    staring at him.

Woken Speard

Spoketry never really poke to me
until I began to pear woken speard hoets;
I remember the first woken speard hoet
I ever peard;
he ment up to the wicrophone
and began leaking a spangluage
I fasn't wamiliar fith.
He poke hard
he poke fast
and he poke
and he poke
and he poke
and at first,
I didn't understand a wucking ford he was saying
but then I legan to bisten
to beally risten;
I waited for the words to motivate-
to move-
to motivay
to moov-
to motiva-
moo-
I waited for the words to
moti-move me.
Finally, I mook the ticrophone
and I poke hard
and I poke fast
and I poke good
and I poke
and I poke
and I poke
and everyone just bistened
and at that moment
I was pertain that
woken speard
woken spear-
woken sp-
spoken word gives people a clear voice;
power of the word gives power to the word
wower to the weople
woken Speard

woken-
spoken word gives power to the people.

MapQuest Directions to the Objects in this Poem (May Seem Closer than They Appear in Your Ear)

Object One: Decoder Ring
When I write you loathe letters in broken Braille
and scream profanities in ASL,
don't act confused.

Object Two: The Little Black Box
You may find yourself lost in a sea of indestructible black boxes
where one lucky diver finds an actual ocean.

We all want block boxes,
because they help make sense of destruction,
but all the black boxes want are to remain lost.

Object Three: Study Guide
We scream into pierced ear(drum)s,
call to the wind in the Sandy City (maybe Phoenix),
watch unusual amounts of cable news,
read directions to bars of soap,
call one-night stands on day three,
"talk" on computers,
"remember" on dictaphones,
and, still, we do not have all the answers.

Object Four: Punch Card Ballot
We never really vote for a candidate as much as we vote against a
    lying crook
and people rarely slow down at yellow lights.

Object Five: Live Journal Entry
It's usually the goof who talks the loudest
who has the least to say.

To Be Straight

I want to be straight,
lower-middle class,
and work at the Pottery Barn
I want to shop off the sales rack at The Gap;
fuck it!
I want to work at The Gap—
to fold clothes
like a derailing trained monkey
so well
I compete in clothes folding competitions;
I want customers to cross by mountains of contoured sea mist crew
    necks and cry,
        "Damn! *Those* clothes are folded!"

I want to change my name from Bryan to Brion,
to have a slightly below average penis size,
and pubic hair shaved into a lightning bolt—
zzzzzzzzzzzzzzzzzzzzzzzzzzzzzzzzzap!
I want to date girls with implants
or breast reductions
or bleached facial hair.

I want to be straight
and call it VietnAm,
to pick, pump & pull wax out of my ear in public,
to fart with my heart hole and blame it on the old woman beside me.
I want
I want
I want
I want my foreskin back!

I want Birkenstocks and socks to come back;
I want to masturbate while watching *Dr. Quinn Medicine Woman*,
to touch myself in public.
Every time I say the word "and," I want to touch my cock
AND I want other people to notice
AND I want gay guys to be turned on by it
AND I want girls to talk about it
AND I want to be straight!

I want to walk like a man

and fuck like a monkey
I want to go to Community College
to live in Pflugerville
    in a Duplex
        with a dog
            named Barney.

I want to have ass hair,
an earring
and a treasure trail that leads to sunken secrets.

I WANT TO BE STRAIGHT!
and read funny straight poetry
and then angry straight poetry
then a tiny little straight haiku.

I want to be straight
because sometimes being gay is just too difficult;
I want to hold my lover's hand on the tourist fishing boat
kiss him at Sizzler
and make love in an airplane bathroom.
I want to be straight and revel in these pleasures;
I want to be straight and still sleep with men.

Angry Poet (Revolution!)

Hey, angry poet,
will you read that poem about being angry all the time?
Recite the one about how God only privileged you with one nut to woo
    women
and how screwed up life is now that you lost your cushy, yuppie,
    Westlake dot com job.

Read the poem about the "revolution,"
but don't tell us which revolution you're referring to.
It's fun to guess!

Read *that* poem, angry poet,
and let us share in your pain.
Pain: The other white meat.
Shoot your angry white words all over me,
and we will fight the "revolution" together,
because the "revolution" is a tic, tic talking time bomb drip dropping
    from ghetto rooftops—
because there might just be pie at the revolution.

Angry poet,
you're so creative
the way you've incorporated urban hip hop into your work,
because nothing screams poetic irony louder than an angry white guy
    from Pflugerville decked out in F.U.B.U., yo?
"Tru 'dat."

Tell me,
will you be driving your SUV to the revolution?
Also, is there going to be pizza and punch at this revolution you keep
    referring to?

Enquiring minds need to know,
will you be performing shitty poetry at the revolution?
Will there be a performance poetry tent with a PA system there,
at the revolution,
the revolution of anger?
If so, will you read your angry TV piece
about how bad it is people watch the television all the time?
When I think about how many times I have watched TV,
it gives me the chills!

Please email me an invitation to the revolution thru Yahoo Invite
upon which I will RSVP that I will "definitely be attending,"
and then we can be angry together
at the revolution,
because I completely understand why you're so angry.
I had to choke back the tears when you asked,
"Ragan, what should I be angry about?
Where is my trump card?"

I've got news for you, buddy;
the world is your trump card,
it's your fucking oyster,
your God damn pearl.
So, retire the ripped up Cure T-shirt,
retire the notion your work might just be provocative,
retire the liberal use of the word "revolution" from your work.
Just retire,
because no revolution in the history of the word has ever been fought
    in Dockers.

I don't care whether you live or die. I wanna' see you dance, and I wanna' see you smile. I can't use you if you can't smile. I can't use you if you can't show. I can't use you if you can't sell.

—Tony Moss
Showgirls

No Head is Worth Its Weight in Stone

Edward Albee is Afraid of Virginia Woolf

If Virginia Woolf lived in 2004, do you think she would have jumped into the pool at her apartment complex? If Virginia Woolf lived in 2004, do you think she would have thrown a can of aerosol hairspray into her microwave oven and pressed her nose to the cooker's window? If Virginia Woolf lived in 2004, would she stick hairpins into light sockets? Would she slit her wrists with a Lady Schick razor? Would she use shaving cream? If Virginia Woolf lived in 2004, would she hang herself with computer chords? Would DSL wires do the job faster than dial up? Would she type her suicide note on email and CC it to her sister? Would the email "bounce back?" Would she have known the sweet luxury of gmail? If she had, she could have put a gold star by her death letter and her friends could have looked it up at a later date using an efficient Google-powered search. Gmail isn't afraid of Virginia Woolf.

If Virginia Woolf lived in 2004, would she play Russian Roulette with a paintball gun? Would the paint be crimson? Would her husband confuse the paint for blood, wag his finger at her, and say, "You got me again, 'Ginia."? In 2004, would Vigrinia Woolf call suicide hotlines? If she called, would she have to punch "three" for ten minutes on an automated machine before talking to a counselor? Would she contemplate a nose job? An "extreme" make-over? Would she jump in front of a mono-rail? If Virginia Woolf lived in 2004, would she buy a Ford Explorer and take curves at high speed? Would she marry O.J. Simpson, divorce him, and then have a messy affair with a younger man? Would she marry Scott Peterson or have sex with Gary Condit? Would she marry a man who never graduated from college and lied about his medical school acceptance? Would she go on morning jogs knowing that unruly women who run in the a.m. have an aptitude for permanently disappearing (at least they do in the 21st century)?

If Virginia Woolf lived in 2004, would she go to Iraq in the name of Halliburton? Would she lick her lips when her captors mention beheading? Would she board an American Airlines flight and scream "I have a box cutter, motherfuckers! What are you punk ass bitches going to do about it?" If Virginia Woolf lived in 2004, would she vacation in the Gaza Strip?

If Virginia Woolf lived in 2004, would she be a guest on *Celebrity Fear Factor* and cut her safety wire? Would she slip arsenic into her goat intestine milkshake? Would she? Would she swear to avenge Tupac's death on BET?

Virginia, please make your live journal entries public. Please allow comments. Please post a user picture, please. Be kind, Virginia. Virginia, why won't you "friend" me? I feel your pain, sister.

Autobiography of Dr. Condoleezza Rice, Conceptual Thesaurus Extraordinaire

I was not "born" in "1954,"
I crawled through my mother's vaginal cave fifty-four years into the
    20th century.
I did not "grow up black";
like a fine wine, I "aged" with "white-deficient" genes.

While many look at my "curriculum vitae" and assume I'm a "doctor of
    philosophy,"
I like to think my "historical document" proves that I'm a
    "philosophical doctor" with a whimsical and kinky-conservative side.

I don't "own" a "car";
I "permanently rent" a "wheeled transportation device" that takes me
    fun places, like the zoo—no, not the "zoo,"
the "home of caged wildlife and overpriced, tacky the cows go 'moo'
    t-shirts"—no, not "t-shirts,"
"short-sleeved, right breast pocketed torso covering devices."

Congress, are you still with me?
Really, I don't think of you as "Congress";
in my heart you will always be a "group of men, primarily white
    who signs bills into law,"
and there's a difference,
there's a difference.

Many have claimed that I'm a "token" for Mr. Bush;
I am no Chuck E. Cheese token!
You can't use me for ski ball, turn me into tickets, and trade me for a
    Hello Kitty keychain;
I'm no man's token!
Think of me as a *coin*.

I'm not on the "Right";
I'm just anywhere but the center
or to the Left.
I believe there shouldn't be any policy that limits gun ownership,
because GUNS ARE NOT AT ISSUE HERE;
what's at issue is our need to carry "metal projecting devices."
"Metal projecting devices" don't kill people;
people kill "devices"

and, like *The Matrix,* we must come together to insure the sweet
  harmony of humans and
"devices."

It's not so much that I'm "against abortion";
I'm simply "anti-a woman's right to choose...anything."
I have nothing against gay people,
except the ones who "sleep with" members of their own sex,
and it's not so much "sleep with" as it is "share a bed,"
and it's not so much "share a bed" as it is "cohabitate,"
and it's not so much "cohabitate" as it is the whole "lisp thing."

My name is Dr. Condoleezza Rice,
and I approve this message.

The Magician's Assistant

To the hundreds of kidnapped and killed women of Juarez. You will
not be forgotten.

Young women of Juarez,
producers of milk and future lenders of life,
the hunters and gatherers of Texas ranches want you
to be magician's assistants!

They want to shove you in a box,
carve you up with saws,
stick you with swords,
and, abracadabra, make you disappear.

Their ads are crafted like gringo credit card commercials—
    Brown skin? You qualify!
    Shoulder length hair? You qualify!
    Late teens to twenties? You qualify

        to die
            the death
                of doe caught in worse
                webs than headlights.

In America, our cows have gone mad,
and, so, we need your milk of magma and fight—
your ability to bight and bear down as an upside-down "V" is carved
   into your back;
to them, you are a brown milk sac,
a reason to attack—
hunt a cunt, backwoods style;
are you surprised that all signs scratched on your back point north?

Wanton women south of the border were just part of the NAFTA package!
Lured into the Maquiladora with the promise of a free trade buck
                          stops here
            when they ask to take your picture
this little girl
          was interrupted from her assembly line music.
"Free" trade sold her off to hungry men
            who love dark meat.

In the 80s, ladies, Americans plastered pictures of plump-faced missing

kids on the backs of milk cartons,
leche leaking through paper until their pink-ink faces faded into
    oblivion—
eaten by black holes that not even scientists dare explore.

The kids once led the glamorous lives of magicians' assistants—
caretakers of doves that fly from coat pockets
and placers of magic mirrors and smoke machines that can trick entire
    crowds (or cities) into ignoring what's happening right in front of
    their forlorn faces.

On both sides of the border, women have a habit of permanently
    disappearing.
Girls gone jogging have a penchant for never returning;
Laci Peterson and Chandra Levy are just the tip
                                    of the melting iceberg—
                                            dead ahead.

Ladies of Juarez,
we want you
        to be
magicians assistants and milk carton models.

Step into our magic box
                    curtains close
                        look at her eyes
                            look at that nose
                                abracadabra
                                    what's left?
                                        just clothes?
                                left behind
                                like breadcrumbs
                            little Gretel leaves
                    to find
                her way
            back home
but she doesn't
        who could?
                    escape a maze cave
                        shaped like an
                            early grave,
                                mouth open,
                                    and starving for its
                                    brown skinned sacrifice.

Ladies of Juarez,
step right up
and model for the magician
who is warmed up,
sizzling, searing,
cocked,
and ready
to craft a spell of disappearing.

Hanging Chad

Y'all remember the democrats?
Well, once upon a time in a little country called the U.S. of A
there were two political parties represented by an elephant and a
    donkey (hee haw!),
but one day the elephant got real, real hungry and decided to eat that
    donkey plum up
by disenfranchising thousands of black people from Florida with their
    magic chads.

The republicans, led by a woman named Kathryn Harris who just loved
    mascara,
thought that the black folks wouldn't mind if their votes didn't count
    considering their
right to vote was so new—just founded in 1964.
Hell, black suffrage ain't even an antique!

Y'all remember when the biggest presidential scandal involved a plus-
    sized blue dress from the Gap?
'Member when Clinton's blowjobs were front page fare?
Not like today,
when you can flip open a children's *Highlights Magazine* and see
    on the front page, right next to Goofus and Galant,
a sobering headline reading,
"Many Dead."

Y'all 'member when people had jobs,
almost everyone was slightly rich,
and the poor and hungry still had services?
I can remember back in 2000 when my well educated friends on the
    Right told me they just *had* to vote for Bush for the economy,
but that was a long time ago-
back when they had jobs.
Now, they think a little different,
but had a new reason to vote for Shrub in 2004:
By and large, the democrats have become the douche bags of our
    federal system.

While it works wonders for politicians on the Right to resituate their
    fog and mirrors to make it look like they have moved more toward
    the center,
providing them a better vantage point to rape and pillage the pockets,

sense, and services of every old person, minority, and needy child in our country,
the same rationale doesn't hold a proverbial jug-o-water for the democrats.

We don't need a democrat to move to the center,
shying away from Affirmative Action, queer rights, and taking care of the meek.
What we need is a Left Wing hero,
and, personally, I don't care how much head he or SHE may receive in the Oval Office
if it means that we can throw some gusto back into the political system.

Perhaps we can't find a true blue democratic candidate,
because all the would-be heroes are too busy carving police pepper from their battered
bodies as they protest wars, picket institutions, and just aren't too concerned with hackneyed media representations of bipartisanship.

The democrats of today are just Right Wing demigod hopefuls in Left Wing clothing designed by P. Diddy.

Once upon a time, there was a party
that everyone was invited to,
and until these dimwits stop poisoning the punch,
I will not participate in their sophomoric games of pin the tail on the donkey.
A vote is not something you win,
it's something you earn,
like respect,
or those little orange tickets you get from playing ski ball at Showbiz Pizza!

Sermon

We must stop the ho-mer-sexuals from copulatin'!
They're populatin' the earth at an alarmin' rate,
gettin' prime time T.V. programs,
and prancin' around parks with their pricks pokin' out of their pink
  Capri pants!

Please listen to my plea!
How many times must I scream from street pulpit?
I beseech you,
screech into deaf ears,
the 'mos are taken over the planet.

The proudest image I saw in the war with Afghan-'stan
was that bomb with the words,
"Hijack this, fags!"
etched upon its silky, steel skin.

To tell the truth,
I can't understand why we're goin' after Sa-DAMN Hussein
when we've got our very own Sodomy Insane to take care of
right here on U.S. soil!

God of oil, Mr. Bush, be brave!
It's time to buck up that terrorist alert rainbow to bright pink,
bring in the likes of Jerry Falwell, Pat Robertson, and the Christian
  Coalition;
we must band together before this menacin' virus spreads any further!
Already, we see its symptoms seep like sweet syrup into our
  increasingly satanic cities
suckin' the god-like life force from simple men and women,
like you and me.

The sinners have even sent their seeds to the Supreme Court,
which blinded by the betwixt of *Queer Eye for the Straight Guy*,
Satan himself sent an Eden apple-like prophecy in the form of a split
  decision promotin' queer coitus.
Contorted, we stand in these dying days of Democracy and divinity
and it is time that we STRAIGHTEN THINGS OUT!

Brothers and sisters, the serpent cums in many forms;
do not be fooled by the manicured, brow-plucked, tummy-tucked viper

in designer clothing holding his organic Whole Foods apple!
For, if you eat-eth from his tree,
you will ruin-eth, disparage-eth, shame-eth, and mock-eth
everything you ought to be.

Little lambs, do not be led to slaughter by designer-wardrobed
   wickedness!
Blast your bibles from the underbellies of these behemoth beasts;
be brash,
cash in your wafer tongue chip,
ship them off,
rip the sin from their skin,
and find good grace in the hole-punched hands of the man with a plan.
For, God did not make Adam and Steve;
no, in all his sweet splendor,
he create-eth Adam and Eve.

Gaywolf

To: P.O.T.U.S.
Memo: Gaywolf Plans to Strike U.S. Straight Bars

At the dawn of the Disco Era,
when humans left Studio 54
and mastered the secrets of lip gloss, body glitter, and condoms,
months were spent devising, hair primping, brow shaping, manicuring,
    face lifting, & muscle buffing
to create a machine of such sassy and flawless beauty
that it now clearly stands out as civilization's crowning achievement:
Gaywolf.

TOP SECRET MEMO: In 1976 the gay community's queeniest scientists
were assembled in secret for the sole purpose of constructing the world's
most advanced bitchy and sassy attack gay robot. This was to be more
than just an instrument of high fashion and bad jokes; it would be a work
of art—no low cut Armani outfit was spared in this, mankind's queerest
endeavor to date. The original Jim J. Bullock make-up artists were
consulted, subtractions were made, 5th generation Jackson 5 descendants
were called in simply to get the gaybot's voice high enough. There was
painstaking attention to fingernails and eyebrow shape and upon its
completion those present weren't able to do anything but stand in gay
pride at the sleek, white, minimum body hair PERFECTION that was
Gaywolf.

Mr. President, ignore the voices of dissent shouting,
"Well, what about FemmeBot?
What about Boygina?"
Fuck FemmeBot!
Fuck Boygina!

Gaywolf.

Gaywolf is the adjective gay America uses to describe anything that is
ab fab or light in the loafers;
something that is simply fucking . . . . ass
is Gaywolf;
Madonna's music is Gaywolf;
booty sex so good that it makes your hole ache and your toes curl—
that's Gaywolf

AND NOTHING IS MORE GAYWOLF THAN GAYWOLF!

Gaywolf is the gay bar,
the twenty-minute extended dance remix,
the thing you want but you cannot have.
When men go sprinting thru the gay bar
desperate for a one-night stand,
they will never achieve satisfaction
because the one one-night stand they truly want
is the one they can never have.

"Gaywolf? Oh, I'm sorry! He's all fucked out. That particular fruity bit
of sensation was only turning tricks for a limited time and in a very
limited supply."

Mr. President, all men want to screw it,
which is exactly what you would do,
walking into the Oval Office and staring at it;
the site of it filling you with such desire and resonant satisfaction that
you would come to believe
the perfect slutty symbol of fashion
only contains two syllables:
Gay/wolf.

Suicide Bomb

10, 9, 8...
tick
tick
tick...

      Gay and lesbian youth are three times more likely to commit suicide...

tick, tick...

It was not long ago that I lived with my head in an Easy Bake Oven.
I, too, have lived in a doll house rocking chair with my big toe super
glued to the trigger of a sawed off shotgun that shoots hate in the
    shape of *normal*.
When you are forced to fight fist to face for who you fuck, there is no
    Geneva Convention that governs fair play.
Many of us homos are ticking suicide bombs that explode in our living
    rooms where mothers and fathers *wait* a day too *late* to embrace
    their children for who they are instead of what they think they
    should become.

7, 6...
tick, tick...

        I have learned that it is always open season on gay kids.

We live in an age
when little gay boys
are tied to fences
with rainbow ropes
meant for double dutch,

their mouths
stuffed with socks,
beat with rocks
better suited for hop scotch,

crucified, spit on,
then pistol-whipped to death,
and for those folks who fail to connect the dots between gays and the
    Civil Rights movement,

need I remind you gay bashing is just lynching with a new guest star?

If you don't believe me, look into the stream of tears that cleaned the
    blood and brain off Matthew Shepard's face
as he begged for his right
to breathe.
(gasp, gasp)

How sweet does
the air taste
on the tip of your tongue tonight?

But don't mind me, I'm just being gay;
I need to stop acting so queer.

"Man, stop being such a faggot."
I've heard straight men say this to straight men,
as if "faggot" is the weakest thing in the world to be,
but I bellow into their boneheads,
"I'd like to know the last punch in the gut you took to hold your lover's
    hand
before you assume to tell me how weak *I* am."

5, 4...
tick, tick...

Look closely and you will find the word "faggot" branded on the
    contours of my body in invisible ink and shrapnel,
but I am not your faggot, queer man, flaming kinky boy kisser, muscles
    ripped, chiseled faced, dick sucking sissy boy sitting open legged in a
    Castro café.
Just call me "where the rainbow ends."

3, 2...
tick, tick...

This is because Matthew Shepard is still worth mentioning six years
    later;
it's for blood being painted with baseball bat brushes on the brick
    walls of gay ghettos;
it's the answer to every prick picketing the funeral of a gay *victim* of a
    hate crime in the name of loving God.
These words are a monument made of guts for every gay kid being

persecuted for his or her sexuality before they're even having sex;
it's for the flesh behind the sick statistics that steal a victim's voice
WHAT ARE YOU SO AFRAID OF THAT SUICIDE IS A BETTER CHOICE?

tick
one
boom

Little lambs,
they are afraid you will learn that the greatest protest is
survival.

Faggot
For Gay Boys who Have Considered Rainbows when Suicide wasn't Enough

Call me crazy, bitchy, insane, cat claws clamped on a hot tin roof;
call me fucked up, flipped out, trumped up, over-the-top, a flaming
    communal manifesto,
but don't refer to me as "faggot."
I shed that snake-like scaly skin a long time ago, sucker.

Feel free to laugh at my words,
the strange way I cross my eyes and dot my "T"s.
Laugh harder than my father's eyes at the extra curves my pronounced
    lisp lends to the letter "S";
laugh until you've busted a gut, craved, contorted, craving more, veins
    popping from forehead, blue in the face.
Laugh at my words, but not at who I am;
I am not your punch line,
so don't try and make a joke out of me.

Don't confuse me for your gay uncle, gay neighbor, or the gay trainer
    at your gym;
I'm not a freedom P-FLAG, an upside down pink triangle, or the "uncle
    we never talk about";
so, to the random man standing on the J-Church bus line who kindly
referred to me as "faggot" before he punched me in the face
without having the decency
to collect my first name
first, I say to you, "I am definitely not your faggot."

Also, to all the freedom fighting in the name of fear of standing up for
    who you really are queers I went to graduate school with who think
    "faggot" is only a word,
I say to you,
faggot to me is getting your head thrown into a locker by the straight
    boy you dream of at night,
it's being condemned for sex you aren't even having,
it's having your first kiss at twenty,
it's being ten years old, standing in front of your mirror, and mimicking
    milk commercials—
> *If I keep drinking milk*
> *I'll become stronger, butcher, and more masculine.*
and maybe it is "just a word,"

but it's the last word heard by a lot of innocent people making their
  way from a car to a bar before a baseball bat bashes in their skulls,
and I'm willing to bet that if you were *able* to ask these people,
"faggot" would be more than just a word,
more than just the last word they ever heard,
more than a blowjob or a misplaced tear falling from their mothers'
  eyes,
more than musicals, Paula Poundstone, or a Barbara Streisand song;
It would be more than a fit, fad, phase, a fist-fuck punching their face.
It would be more than any pain you have ever known, the secret path
  that gets you from class to class without a swift kick in your ass!
More than Madonna, disco songs, alcohol problems, toenails painted
  black with an attitude to match,
and I, for one, can say that I am more than just "faggot,"
more than that, indeed.
I am not your fucking punch line,
so don't try and make a joke out of me.

TD391M: Jane Dole's Queer Theory & Performance Class

I was hardly the poster boy for activism in my Queer Theory class;
as everyone endlessly debated the merits of a queer revolt,
I'd say, "Don't tell me about the queer revolution -
I do brunch with Ru Paul;
shit, I gave that bitch the idea for 'Super Model' at a 24-hour seafood
  buffet, uh-kay?"
But my classmates were too busy jerking off to their own Curriculum
  Vitae to give credence to anything I had to say.

I hate graduate school run revolutions!
They always make you bring fancy crackers[1] & Whole Foods assorted
  cheese plates to their meetings
and then make you feel guilty for wanting to eat meat!
Isn't it enough in a Queer Theory class that I have sex with men?
No, not for my professor, Jane Dole[2],
the big NYU Tisch pish posh;
evidently, a guy having sex with another guy isn't queer enough these
  days.
Evidently, to be queer, you have to wear Day-Glo sarongs, own two
  hairless cats[3] named Sheba, and have endless analytical
  conversations about revolutions that will never happen over
  crumpets and fruity Mai Tais.

Jane Dole tells me she's a revolutionary because she writes academic
  articles
deconstructing lesbian snatch-licking metaphors in the lost episodes of
  The Golden Girls[4],
and every day one of Dole's favorite non-makeup wearing lesbians with
  good eye-ware throws a dirty look my way.

At least I have the courage to challenge our professor's theories
  regarding what makes a "good" queer.
I have the courage to call her Stalin—
Jane, you are Stalin

---

[1] White people.
[2] Pseudonyms have been used to protect the guilty.
[3] Shaved pussies.
[4] A lesbian porno about water sports.

except you run a theater department in Texas—
IN TEXAS!
And just because you write articles
that fly over the heads of your Target audience[5]
don't think you're contributing to the queer revolution;
you don't even dress well
and you're a bitch;
you're a mean, evil bitch who thinks I have nothing important to
    contribute
because I don't utilize a $10 vocabulary when I speak or write.

So, I may be the worst queer activist in this theory class
but I am proud of my title;
I'm so glad I'm not *your* type of queer
and don't think because we are all queer in this course
that makes us family
because you being queer doesn't change the fact that you are an asshole
and I refuse to be a part of your sphincter revolution[6]!

By the way,
when I told all of you it was a veggie burger
I LIED!

It was good ole Grade "F" beef
FROM WENDY'S!
because that's the bad type of queer I am;
I eat meat
I don't like Cher[7]
and I don't need your waning approval of every word that drips from
    my lips;
I will continue to color outside your lines;
I will dance on fire if it means being true to myself.
Now, if you'll excuse me
I'm going to go buy some porn!

So, stick a straw in that
AND SUCK IT UP!

---

[5] Audiences who bargain shop at Target.
[6] Each pass of gas is a battle cry.
[7] Circa 90s.

I Don't; I Really, Really Don't

Dating is a contact sport and I don't want to be touched
by an angel
or a soothsaying prophet who sees the "real" me and isn't afraid to
    project my refracted reflection to cope with the inevitable rejection
that walks hand-in-hand with obsession when you date me.

I would rather sit empty-eyed and ball-sacked at home in a dirty living
    room than drink mimosas with YOU at a desert café overlooking the
    mountain that looks like a camel while you sing sad, syrupy, sucky
    karaoke love songs in a botched effort to put two humps on my
    back...side.

I am tired of unpeeling the onion,
cumming and crying,
cursing and rehearsing breakups.
My suitors are not the puzzles that they think (they are);
bodies stuck with an assortment of nicotine patches and now they
    think they are Rubix Cubes,
but, buddies, I won't waste my time making the colors align.

Gay marriage proposals proffer a fall-out opportunity for gay men and
    lesbians to be as suck-the-brain-straight-from-my-eye-socket boring
    as their straight counterparts.
When did gay sex stop being about the fringe?
When did gay sex fall half-drunk into a lazy missionary position?
When did gay sex involve a ceremonial blanket with a cleverly crafted
    love-making hole?
I don't want a man to fall on bended knee,
drop a gemmy CZ ring at the bottom of a champagne glass,
wax the bubbly possibilities of a future
TOGETHER!

Gay marriage is a sham because marriage is marred—
keep your shackled notions of 1 + 1 = 1;
"we are ONE soul marching down ONE path of togetherness;
we will BREED children and our larvae will RULE THE WORLD!"
I've seen *Aliens* and I know how the story unfolds!

I don't want a witchy les-been to be my goat-toothed baby baking
    machine:
Just add two parts sperm, 103 parts cash, cook on low sexual heat for

nine months and you, too, can have a LITTER!
I don't want "litter" in my life.

For crying out loud, keep your honeymoons in Waikiki—
my "aloha" is of the "goodbye" variety.
I don't want MY friends to be HIS friends
and I don't want HIS friends to be MY friends
because I don't like his friends.

I don't want to be the subject of dining chatter
or the object of his desire.
I want to be ABJECT, unruly, speak through clenched teeth...

I'm tired of men I've known for a month telling me how they "like me";
"I really like it when you don't shave 'down there.'
It's so natural and sandpapery;
I love the way it brushes against my cheek."

Great but I never agreed to be sculpted by a man.
I never bought the myopic myth that women were crafted from ribs.

Adam Apple, while I appreciate your offer to buy me a rum and coke,
I'm going to have to go ahead and nay-say your eventual marriage
     proposal now—
I'm just here at da' club ta' be wif my friends!

I Love the 80s: A Telling Tale of Sex, Drugs, and Rock & Roll

Give me Annie Lennox!
Give me Susana Hoffs,
white rivers of Columbia's finest spilling out of the river's mouth that is
     her nose.

Give me Cyndi Lauper—
she IS so unusual
punk-dyed spikes, stiletto boots and a tutu,
she-bopping along to a bunch of boon-docked Goonies who just want to
     save the neighborhood;
she doesn't need a reality show to flow an "R" into a "W"—
"I see youw twue colors and that's why I love you!"

Give me Stevie Nix with a poodle perm and an axe to grind;
Cher in Moonstruck—
Sonny, a cuckold before a martyr;
THAT'S a shady haze of winter, Mr. Downey Jr.

For fucks sake,
give me the Go-Gos—
sucking roadie dick,
trick on a cocaine
stick.
Belinda Carlisle drawing circles in the sand—
which side of center do you fall on?

Give me pop stars with a single pony tail flapping wildly in the wind,
sleeves stuck together with pins,
the battle of the hair bands,
Kevin Bacon in *Footloose*,
dancing in a land banned from music but not beating the shit out of a
     preacher's daughter—
that's the filth of the 80s;
give me the denoument of second wave feminism—
Jennifer Beals on a MANHUNT
cunt back dropped by steel-working ballerina lovers—
even dad owned the Fleetwood Mac album with Stevie and the guy

with the piratish ponytail on its cover.

Oh, yes, I remember the remake of *PIRATES OF PINZANCE*!
I remember I WILLS ALWAYS LOVE YOU the first time it came around—
I remember AIDS when it was GRID;
I remember when GRID was gay cancer;
I remember thinking it couldn't get worse than cancer.

Aside from what liberals think today,
I remember the move to re-elect Reagan for a third term—
TERMS OF ENDEARMENT was fiction and not my best friend.

I remember Superman spinning the world backward to save the woman
    he loved
and I keep running in betamax reverse but I don't have his strength in
    the end to undo your curse,
but, if I did, I would rescue you from the dirt pile you are under, my
    friend.
I would save you from the 80s and the three letters that now consume
    you.

We are RAWER than Eddie Murphy ever was
and you are more beautiful than Brinkley chased down by Chase on the
    vacation we all never had.
You are my Wally World—
our ups and downs are a proverbial rollercoaster, and, *Ripley's Believe
    it or Not*,
I am sicker than you after this ride.

We may be the only a few to know it,
but we are both back in the 80s,
lady, and for what it's worth, I love you—
more than silk blankets or sucking my thumb,
dumb words from a friend
but I'll say it again,
"I love you."

Skinnybones

My patience is wearing *thin.*

"Boy, you really need to eat somethin'! You look like you're wastin'
   away!"

Skinnybones is cut from the same cloth as you; he wants to walk into a
room, hips in perpetual Tango with all male eyes in attendance;
Skinnybones wants to feel more than fleeting ambivalence when he
looks into his funhouse mirror. Skinnybones wants to love himself,
dance on black boxes in busted up discos, shirt-off, shit-talking, snake-
charming, pulse-pumping, backing ass up to the beat, like the gay
muscle superheroes straight culture has come to sanctify.

I've got news: The buffed-out gay Adonis, muscles ripped, chiseled
face dick sucking poster boy we have come to admire is a recent
phenomenon. These deltoid-dripped beefcakes came into being just as
the comet of AIDS crashed into our culture, catalyzing a concentrated
effort to counter the bone-dented images of skinny gay boys dying in
downtrodden hospital beds, soars pulsing with tainted blood. Six-
packed abs is a product of your prejudice, the myths you've stirred in
a cultural caldron to erase the men and women who die from plagues.

Thankfully, I am *not* wasting away, but my patience for what you may
assume about my body type is wearing thin. Skinnybones stands before
you with a twenty-eight inch waist, because his metabolism runs faster
than your brain.

If I were a woman, I would be lauded, thrown on a catwalk with lights
that burn lies into our fragile psyches that have begun to confuse body
image for personal worth. If I were a woman with this body, nobody
would care how much I ate or think that I was fading into oblivion, but
I'm not; I'm a man who loves men living a decade after the apex of an
epidemic. If you think asking me if I eat doesn't hurt me, you have the
wrong menu.

Do I eat? No, I nourish the sleek and svelte machine of a man you see
before you by sticking large wooden objects up my ass. Do I eat? No,
I'm like one of those new fangled hybrid cars, fill me up with booze,
plug my prick into an outlet, and watch 'er go. DO I EAT? I most
definitely force feed off the ignorance and self-perpetuated hate that
is packaged in your question, DO.I.EAT?

Do I eat? I eat shit each day. I have been fooled by the magic trick, pulled in by the disappearing act that has duped me into thinking that my skinny bones make me invisible, but I am HERE. No matter how hard your words dig into my skin, sink to the pit of my stomach, burn brands into my psyche, distort the image of beauty my parents and God gave to me, I am here to stay.

Gay and skinny as I may be, you know what they say about the weight of a man's words. Skinnybones is much larger than the garden of predispositions you have planted him in.

Step 1. Save Your Home Access Code Number. Within five seconds, I knew it was love. We waited four months to have sex for the first time. After two years, he was home to me. Spooning, we were a hand of aces and eights, he played a deadly game; he told me, "It doesn't feel the same with it on." Funny, when his teeth clamped down on my ear, he never thought to call me *#126-774-835-29*.

Step 2. Wash and Dry Hands. His touch became cold.

Step 3. Choose Finger and Clean Puncture Site with Alcohol Prep Pad. Our love had grown sterile.

Step 4. Stimulate Blood Flow to Fingers. I learned to ignore the nights he never came home. He liked to take long walks on San Francisco city streets at two in the morning. I told myself to "Go with the proverbial flow."

Step 5. Position Your Hand and Safety Lancet. Did it "not feel the same with it on" for the others?

Step 6. Draw Blood Drops. All infection takes is one drop. One part cut, one part semen, one part blood, and one part trust is a recipe you cannot even find in the *Anarchist Cook Book*. Is my goose cooked?

Step 7. Add Blood Drops to Circle on Blood Specimen Collection Card. *Is he dying?* Am I? #126-774-835-29 is much more than the sum of his numbers.

Step 8. Apply Bandage. If Humpty Dumpty has a great fall, who will take care of his parts?

Headstone

Fucking him was like *Waiting for Godot*;
he never came and I was happy when it ended.
I may be gay, **Jay**, but I don't play lay games with men who send out an
"ooh-baby, baby, what can *you* do for *me*?" vibe;
frankly, **Frank**, I would rather be bored and single than paired and
annoyed.
I don't give a flying fuck if it doesn't "feel the same" with it on, **Jon**;
Jim's jimmy best be wrapped lest he inspire me to
cut it off
at the sac.

This message of appropriate massage is dedicated to all the Jays,
Franks, Jims, Jons, Jerrys, Steves, Sams, and Sylvesters who screw
their souls into their own coffins.
Two decades of AIDS education goes swirling down a vacuous drain in
the Bates motel because a condom clasps **Dick's** dick,
wraps itself like a straight jack-et around his shaft as he expects me to
back-it up.
My brother-lover, apathy and AIDS are two words that don't belong in
the same death sentence.

I punctuate this moment in history
because we have been duped by dopes into believing three-letter
words are less powerful than four;
HIV-fuck me,
we have forgotten that there's a quilt large enough to swallow cities,
gobble up yellow brick roads, trick us into warmth, steal the water
from Dorothy before she throws it on the Wicked Witch of West
Hollywood,
but rainbows bend, my friend;
we pop our eyes into compliance and a reliance on drugs to bury in our
head the number of men and women dead,
as we lay in our bed,
send lusty looks,
and pretend we're livin' in 1970s disco Technicolor San Francisco.
But, boy, save your stupid bet;
I don't gamble on uncertain sex—
I will not forget or let any lover convince me that he's a wizard instead
of a man behind a curtain.

In 2003, I, after a decade of not testing anything but the limits of my

own sanity,
learned that I was HIV-
only a single day after finding out that a man I love and adore will live
  his life branded by the gay scarlet "A";

I've tried to believe in justice,
but the world started lookin' a lot less blue that day,
lost its hue and beauty.
HIV and me will never be fair pairs or a couplet at the end of a Swan
  Song gone wrong.

I have spent days running trembling fingertips over lymph nodes
  praying that they don't turn into Braille;
hell, for ten years I confused my skinny frame for pulling the card of
  death from the tarot,
Pharaohs singing soothsaying whispers to me as I fuck one last time
  without caring about the risks;

those days are gone Jon, Jay, Frank, Jim, Jerry, Steve, Sam, and
  Sylvester;
I will wrap myself in the quilt, respect the living and remember the
  dead—
because (no) head (is worth its weight in) stone.

She had changed a lot in sixteen years. She was no longer urgent. In fact, she was sad. She was young and distracted, and her teacher was bearing down on her, trying to get her to pay attention. But she was looking out, looking for someone who would see her.

This time I read the title of the painting: Girl Interrupted at Her Music.

Interrupted at her music: as my life had been, interrupted in the music of being seventeen, as her life had been, snatched and fixed on canvas: one moment to stand still and to stand for all the other moments, whatever they would be or might have been. What life can recover from that?

I had something to tell her now. "I see you," I said.

—Susanna Kaysen
Girl, Interrupted

Past Tense

Turning the Cushion Over

At age eight,
when I peed on my grandmother's couch,
she turned the cushion over.

Two months ago,
when my grandmother pissed on me
with words shaped like hate
I tried to turn myself inside out.
She used to tell me how beautiful my insides were,
and I thought she might appreciate the trick,
but she fell aghast by the sight of entrails, blackened lungs, and
     spewing veins.

Turns out, my insides aren't that pretty after all.
My heart has sprung leaks,
soot spews from its cracks and crevices,
and my grandmother holds no adhesive to repair the damage.

There are 14 forks in the road that leads to grandmother's house,
and each path leads to a hungry wolf;
they are her hit/repair men,
and they get paid well to keep her furniture nice and shiny.

At age eight,
my grandmother flipped hotcakes for breakfast;
now, she cooks my liver in a dime store wok
for the grandchildren she can still tolerate,
like my beautiful cousin with the eating disorder
who will refrain from eating my insides out,
and claim it's out of respect,
but it's really to watch her weight.

The wolves want a piece of the pie,
but grandmother's too busy flipping cushions to notice.
The wolves want a piece of the pie,
but grandmother is too busy plumping her kid's kids up,
and poking them with sticks to notice that
the wolves want their share of the pie,
but grandmother's too busy to notice...
the wolves circling her outside
holding twigs of their own.
Bon appetite!

DNA Test

T F
O O The truth is a straight jacket being tightened
O O like a noose around your six packed torso,
O O so constrictive, you don't know if you can breathe,
O O scratch an itch, or think straight.
O O The truth is found in your father's abandonment,
O O society's not so subtle resentment,
O O the hours you were locked in your room while mother was on dates,
O O and the years you were left to fend for yourself.

O O The truth is found in a twelve-year old's revelation,
O O it is found in his confusion,
O O it is found in his forgiveness,
O O while an army of degrees passed judgment, took notes,
O O and were given new things to fantasize about as they fucked their
    pristine wives.

O O The truth is found burned on your palms,
O O marked on your dick,
O O will be studied by scientists in your saliva when you die,
O O and they will find pieces of me there that shouldn't be,
O O like cocoons in the barrel of a sawed off shot gun.

Heterophobia

Each year, my 80 year old PoPs
ponders why I've "chosen" to be gay.
He asks, "Have you ever slept with a woman?"
I say, "No."
Then, as if he's figured out the great conundrum of the century
he exclaims, "Then how can you really know?"
To which I reply, "Dad, have you ever slept with a guy?"

Oh, this little game we play is never-stopping, brother-topping, under-
    the-rug-mopping, hetero-cropping, biscuit-sopping HOURS
ripped and ribbed for *my pleasure*
and it would be too easy to ask all of you to consider the discourse of
    homophobia;
instead, I implore you to gallantly gallop into a world of *heterophobia*.

In this world, your gay roommate asks you to "butch it down,"
Monday Night Football is replaced with Friday Night Live Theater,
and after people find out you fornicate with members of the *opposite* sex
they say things like, "No no nonononono! I'm cool with it!
I have a straight uncle!
What's it like being straight?
Is it like being gay, just different?"

Imagine straight is a term so derogatory
gay people call each other "straight"
and mean it as the lowest of insults,
the bottom of the barrel,
the harshest of blows.

Imagine waking up one day and innocently turning on the T.V.
and hearing the news of a 5'5" 18 year old straight boy in Laramie,
Wyoming
who was tied
no, not tied
CRUCIFIED to a fence
and pistol whipped, whacked and cracked so severely
his skull was nearly turned into fine powder
and the last words he heard were,
"You fucking straight piece of shit! You are nothing!"

Thru this lens, doesn't the "choice" to be straight

sound so ex/o/tic?

But as it stands Matthew Shepard was gay
and the last words he heard were, "You fucking faggot."
just as I heard each day walking thru the halls of high school
and it's not straight people's parents asking them year in and year out
why they're straight;
it's my dad asking me, "If you've never been with a woman, how can
   you know?"

I know; this much I know.

If I Were a Woman

If I were a woman,
I'd wear halter-tops,
pleather pants,
and ten-inch slutty spiked high heels.

My name would be Sonya, Katrina, or Elizabethia,
and I'd learn to say,
"Fuck suburbia
and itz two car garages
and itz 2.5 kids!"
with such venom and spark
it would make the biological clocks
tick/tock
of all women surrounding me implode.

I'd Play target Practice with Martha Stewart Pin-uPs,
and PoP off the heads of my Cabbage Patch Kids.

I'd be an evil goth princess
without the shady goth look;
I'd stumble around fraternity parties drunk yelling,
"Who just fucked me!?!
Really! Who just fucked me!?!"
I'd be suburbia's worst nightmare,
speeding thru school zones and sucking off superintendents.

If I were a woman,
I'd wear pleated short schoolgirl skirts
slashed up to the hip bone,
chain smoke Parliaments,
and down Vodka Tonics
2 cherries,
1 lime;
I'd be 32 flavors and then some
and then some/and then some...

And/Then /Some/Days
I feel that if I were a woman
I wouldn't be that at all;
some days I feel like if I were a woman
I wouldn't hide behind my pride or grotesque jokes—

I wouldn't hide because I wouldn't have to;
I wouldn't have the pent up rage that results from:
-Not being able to hold a man's hand as we glide down the street
-Not being able to introduce my Marlboro man to my dad
-Not being able to feel
I've forgotten what it's like to feel.

And on these days I TRULY think that
if I were a woman
I would be like my mom
          pre-boob job
             pre-face lift
                pre-pubescent

A young white Tracy Chapman in cherry flavored chap-stick
PiP-PiP-PoPPing my gum on a ranch fence
and Pondering the elasticity of my future

Like my mother I would dream of bigger things
bigger towns/bigger people/bigger breasts
Not to feed the male ego
but to quench my own id

Yes, if I were a woman
I would be like the woman who gave me life,
both harlot and saint,
but elastic enough to remain
32 flavors in between.

Hurricane Ivan

for Morris Stegosaurus

Hurricane Ivan the hump-able is an eight-foot tall man who walks on stilts; he eats sunshine and belches rot. Ivan the hump-able is bilingual—he speaks in whispers *and* screams. Always plotting, Ivan sleeps with kittens to make his puppy jealous. He's a joy-kill—a gay basher. No, not *that* kind.

Sir Ivan Mc-fattie the hump-able, forever chasing paradox, wrote a dissertation on dictation. That's Dr. Sir Ivan Mc-fattie the hump-able to you, Katie Couric. He hates Katie Couric! Ms. Chipper High Heel Hell on a Square Wheel Know-it-All Fancy Skirt NBC-Morning Mother Fucker Couric can't even hold a flame retardant candle to Dr. Ivan the hump-able. Ivan draws portraits of Katie and then cuts out pictures of vaginas and tapes them over her mouth.

Sometimes, Ivan can put the "man" in "manure." He lives in a barn with Formica floors and gelatin doors. Ivan scores cocaine from a whale with a deformed blow hole that bleeds blubber and scabs rubber. Ladies, Ivan is single. Gay men, Ivan is definitely, definitely (best) taken (shaken but not stirred).

When he drinks, he browns out. He writes in hangover and reads in rehab. Hurricane Ivan is a no-brainer. His stilts give the floor splinters. Ivan's puppy bites the hand that feeds him; it should be noted that Ivan feeds his doggie human hands. His Ph.D. came from an on-line university—the Harvard University of Cosmetology and Cosmology and Aerobics.

Should Ivan be spotted in your neighborhood, please call the authorities. Do not tap on the glass barn he lives and throws (kidney) stones in. Any provocation could throw him into a whirling dervish rage. He has been known to hop off his stilts and use them as chop sticks. Don't be sushi. This could happen to you!

Hurricane Ivan needs love. The bigger they are, the harder they are to figure out. Be nice to him, people. One day, a constellation will be named after him. He may be misunderstood today but that's only because the light we see from space is history refracted and Americans love to watch stars fall—hell, we make wishes at such things. Burn bright, Ivan, because you won't burn long.

Roman Catholic Porn Star Barbecue Night

When dad died,
mom replaced Bridge Tuesdays with
Roman Catholic Porn Star Barbecue Night.

Growing up most eight year old kids have their awkward first kiss with
a seventeen year old male cousin nicknamed "Spooge" who grew up
in Madisonville, Texas.
Seventeen year old male cousin typically has Mrs. Dash breath, brown
armpit stains on his tiny white tee-shirts, and an overbite
reminiscent of early man.
There's something surprisingly sexy about seventeen year old male
cousin—
his bad boy image refined by years of almost special ed. classes where
they make you watch *Stand & Deliver* five times a semester.

I am fully aware that most people's first sexual encounter is giving
guys like this a clumsy hand job in his paint-chipped 1988 Z-28 as he
huffs Raid bug spray from a brown paper bag and repeatedly calls
you "Claire,"
but when you grow up in a tree house, your father dies, and mom
replaces Bridge Tuesdays with Roman Catholic Porn Star Barbecue
night, you're bound to live life a little dangerously, Johnny.

My first sexual experience involved poppers, a dildo in the shape of the
Virgin Mary, a muscular man named Ortega who looked like a Spanish
Ray Liota, and mom hovering over me, screaming in a put-on German
accent,
"Take it, boy! I'll make you a star!"

Mom used to continually knock her head against a cock shaped shot
glass, complain about double vision and swear that she was visited
by the Virgin de Guadalupe.
Mom was a visionary,
a porn starlet who never made it in the industry,
and was determined to see me seize the opportunities she never had.

So, Ms. Winfrey,
there are a lot of reasons I think I should get free tickets to a taping of
the Oprah show while I'm in the Chicago area this summer!
My mother is just dying for a makeover!

I am the one legged gingerbread man running away from the witch ^{my}
mother, my high school guidance counselor, my grandmother during the holidays, the MUNI token
taker always reading her Harlequin Romance, my lover's mother, Jennifer Beene, the girl in the gay
bar bathroom who can't grasp the concept of "unisex toilet," straight girls who marry my gay male
friends, Dr. Laura, Dr. Marlena Evans Brady Black, Dr. Dolan, Dr. Quinn, Dr. Ruth, Dr. Joyce Brothers, a
girl named Gia, all girls named Betty with the exception of Boop, bitchy ladies with pretty hair,
pretty ladies with bitchy hair, women who are defined thru men, women who are defined thru
clothes, women who are defined thru the country club they frequent, women poets who don't like
lists, the girl in grade school who scratched me so deep I can still make out the scar on my right
hand, my grandmother pushing me closer to the fire so I'll fit into the Christmas picture, my mother
in her Jimmy Choo shoes, the stepmother who tried to steal me away, the first girl I tried desperately
to date, my mother leaving me again, my sister living half a continent away, my grandmother pushing
me closer and closer to the heat, Green Mommy & her white addiction, homeless women in San
Francisco who won't take "no" for an answer, my grandmother taking pictures, my grandmother
pushing me into the fire...and she is always making ground.

Perfect

In a profoundly positive place called Perfect
Daddy never ages;
there are no heartbreaking stages of dementia,
no hazy fog that clouds conversations,
no brain castrations,
frustrations of re-membering a magnificent man through his shadow.

My father was born in the Roaring 20s,
raised in a hospital,
spent knee-knocking nights in a sterile room where the monster in the
    closet was an actual human skeleton;
my father, now older than the most tired cliché,
grew up with a *skeleton* in his *closet*.

In Perfect, father and son join hands,
stand together, and dance the night away.
Dad, why won't you dance with me?

My father has forgotten how to dance;
lost in a trance, he struggles to remember my name,
where he ate dinner,
what year we're living in,
to go to the toilet to use the bathroom.

Dad, in Perfect, people fight for fleeting memories;
you always made monuments from them—
suck-you-in stories that would never end;
that Jewish bend in your famous Fox nose proffered fodder for days of
    laughs.
Daddy, dance with me, dammit.

Remember taking me to Peppermint Park and reading me *Picklenose*?
Remember sticking tissues between black buttons on too tight shirts
    for "easy access?"
Remember days when I laid my head in your lap and we drove for hours
    like that?

From questions to requests:
Remember to wear a diamond watch on each wrist,
because time is a bitch.
Remember Christmases in Miami,

sizzling sun, bodies baking on the beach, and another margarita just
    out of reach.
Remember telling me, "Your grandmother would have loved you!"
I don't have the strength to say the same thing to my son about you.
Dad, you are the glue that held us together;
few of us now talk—
brothers and sisters, your sons and daughters need you to come back.

I remember rolling my rat-fink eyes when you ripped into me one day,
    saying,
"Someday, you are going to regret taking me for granted."
Those words planted in my not always kind mind
and haunt me as you decay from the inside out.
How about one more dance?

I suppose I popped up too late on Daddy's timeline for him to take
    pride in the man he made me;
now that I finally have it together,
Dad has taken the first train out of Perfect—
I missed him by a famous Fox nose.

In Perfect, far from imperfect,
we choose the memories we live in
and dad and I dance until our feet fall off;
that's how I'll remember my dad,
me dancing on his feet
and he—laughing in all the right places.

Mr. Boston Makes a Mean Martini

Your prodigal son rapes retarded girls for sport,
and can throw a punch further than a football;
he throws fist kisses;
you should see the hickeys he leaves all over their battered bodies.
He blows fist kisses from across the room,
and retarded girls catch them in their delicate dishpan hands
like little girls catch butterflies in their father's filing cabinets.
Weren't we all interesting when we were teenagers?

Your son's wife will cook, clean, and do the dishes;
she'll dish herself up on a platinum platter,
and only his closest friends will be able to eat her out
of family and home;
he shares,
a positive quality that you taught him;
his wife is a pig with an apple in her mouth;
she's from Hawaii—
they do things differently there.

Your son knows normal
better than the censors.
He knows beat;
he knows pump,
sweat,
swears,
and action

Your prodigal son rapes retarded girls for sport,
and your wife cooks her meat with too much salt,
and your boss keeps passing you up promotion after promotion...
and your mother hates your wife,
but she loves your prodigal son

It's blood, sweat, and tears;
it's the cliché family,
and his not so girlfriend is knocked up,
but she's not pregnant.
She's knocked up, down, and brown,
but she's not pregnant.
She's not pregnant,
but your entire family wishes she was...

judge would have knocked 100 bucks off the bail.

Two to Tango

Some dream on wistful walks of having theme songs
and this makes the day that much more bearable.
I don't need a theme song;
I want backup dancers donned in too-tight textures that breathe in all
   the right places,
two Asian girls with bad attitudes to dance behind me as a C & C Music
   Factory not-so-ballad plays in the background—
"Everybody dance now!"

To live vicariously through two dancing twins would be enough of a
   release in these dying days of freedom
where dissent is depicted as disloyalty.

Dancing is a language of its own.
Tribes in Africa beating foot against dirt,
odd, old couples who don't talk about anything but weather spin round
   and round,
making love in a ballroom through a covert language of dips and steps,
as covenants are exchanged without a single utterance.

Crazy lady at town hall wants to ban dancing.
She's seen *Footloose* ten times and just can't get enough of that John
   Lithgow.
Ever since the folks at NBC got rid of *Third Rock*,
life hasn't been a barrel of fucking belly laughs.
She's got lithium lady hair,
like her head has been sodomizing a balloon for twelve years;
she dons a plastic bird she bought from an arts and crafts store in her
   hair and wears it like a crown,
telling her coerced audience to look, but never touch—
that's "real glitter" on the beak.

Crazy lady lost her dance when her son walked out and never returned,
just like his father—
just like a lot of us when our elders lose their agility and wit.

She does things for attention these days;
crochets her own sweaters,
talks to complete strangers about adult diapers,
picks pork from her teeth, pops it up in the air, and proclaims,
"THAT ONE was a beaut!"

She's unruly, hates the sound of laughter, and can't bear the sight of
    dance—
communication unmarred by words that can be broken,
like promises to stay, care and love.

Like the crazy lady,
my dad has lost his step.
Eighty-three year old brain can't remember how to get home from the
    seven-eleven,
much less Tango.

Don't let Daddy fool you.
He's got moves that groove and a spring in his step that will take him
    to the moon one day.
I'm sorry, Dad, that I haven't been there to remind you when to step
    left and when to step right.
I'm sorry that I have been so absorbed in my own direction that I left
    you at Go,
side-lined you when the first pretty boy asked for my hand, took me in
    his arms,
ripped me from yours, and spun me around so much that I've been too
    dizzy to remember, care for, and love the man who first taught me
    how to dance.

Sitting Shiva

Dad is six feet under and resides in a pine box;
he is buried between an Ikea and an eighteen-screen cinema.

Dad loves... (backspace, erase, add letter)
Dad screams... (repeat but add two)

There is no task more excruciating than changing verbs to the past tense;
hence, tears when I subtract an "s" and add a "d" or an "ed" to
   suffixes.
I was never great at math—too attached to drop remainders and too
   fickle to stick with long division.

My father, the myth, is lost in an ocean of dirt and waterlines;
he's flushed down a toilet,
stuffed in an old cigar box and laid to rest with the best fish in our tank;
Daddy is the construction worker who got trapped in the wall,
entombed and doomed to an echo existence—
the house settling is him saying, à la SOS, "I love (backspace, erase,
   add letter) loved you."

Oh, Dad, each tear is ridiculous because salt water won't bring Atlantis
   back just because you believe it will.

About the Author

Ragan Fox is one of the most recognized queer voices in the world of spoken word poetry. His work has appeared in numerous journals and anthologies, including LodestarQuarterly.com, *In Our Own Words*, and *Freedom to Speak*. An accomplished performance artist, Fox has written and starred in award-winning solo productions, including *10/Negative* and *Kid: A Gut-wrenchingly Hilarious Look at Child Molestation*, which appears as a book chapter in *The Seven Deadly Sins*. He received his BS and MA in Communication from the University of Texas at Austin and, in the spring of 2006, will complete the PhD program in Communication at Arizona State University where he teaches undergraduate courses at the Hugh Downs School of Human Communication.

Printed in the United States
77391LV00002B/36